Live Positively
with Ami's Umbrella

Live Positively

with Ami's Umbrella

8 Easy Ways to Jump-Start Your Happiness

by

Ami Ahuja

Live Positively with Ami's Umbrella / 8 Easy Ways to Jump-Start Your Happiness

Published in the United States of America by Essar Enterprises, Inc.

www.AmiAhuja.com / Ami@amiahuja.com

Copyright © 2015 by Ami Ahuja

All rights reserved. No part of this publication may be reproduced, distributed, or transmitted in any form or by any means, including photocopying, recording, or electronic or mechanical methods, without the prior written permission of the publisher or author.

This publication is designed to provide accurate and authoritative information regarding the subject matter covered. It is provided with the understanding that the author/publisher is not engaged in rendering legal, accounting, counseling, or other professional services. If expert assistance is required on any topic herein, it is recommended that the reader seek the services of a competent professional.

Merriam-Webster's Collegiate® Dictionary was consulted for key word definitions provided herein.

This book contains quotes attributed to well-known personalities and other figures. Efforts have been made to ensure the accuracy of the quote and author to whom it is attributed.

ISBN-13: 978-0-9969615-0-9
ISBN-10: 099696150X

Editing by Stephanie J. Beavers Communications

www.StephanieJBeavers.com / 888-823-2283

Dedication

I dedicate this book to my loving husband Sonny Ahuja and my amazing kids Ayesha, Jay, Akarsh, and Alisha. I love each of you with all my heart.

Acknowledgements

I would like to thank my husband Sonny Ahuja for giving me his unconditional love and support. You have always been there for me.

And my lovely, amazing kids—Ayesha, Jay, Akarsh, and Alisha—who always help me when needed.

My life has been an amazing, adventurous roller coaster ride, but I didn't come this far alone. So many others in my life helped me get to where I am today.

I would like to thank my grandparents who bless me from heaven. They taught me the true value of happiness—Maneklal Patel, Savitaben Patel, and Dhayabhai Patel.

I would also like to thank my grandmother Shardaben Patel who lives in Houston, Texas. She always taught me how to be tough and fight it out—and to not take no for an answer.

And of course I thank my parents. They brought me into this world and gave me this amazing life. I have benefited deeply from the love and laughter they share every day.

My mother Ila Patel, a three-time cancer survivor, has always shown strength and taught me to never give up. My father Devdatt Patel has always taught me to be kind and spread my own love and laughter.

I have learned from my mother-in-law Sushma Lal Ahuja to "just aim high and there you have it" and from my father-in-law Dr. Kishan Lal Ahuja to always keep smiling.

I would also like to thank all the members of my "A Woman's Journey" group (www.TheBeautifulWomen.org). They inspire and motivate me to achieve more.

Without the support of everyone who has touched my life, this book would not have been possible.

Contents

Foreword viii
Introduction 1
U *Understand* 3
M *Manage* 8
B *Build* 17
R *Remove* 23
E *Empower* 29
L *Listen* 35
L *Learn* 41
A *Attract* 47
The Big Picture 52

Foreword

I've met thousands of people over the past 30 years—men and women alike, rich and poor, from all professions and walks of life. Whether I was selling, consulting, presenting, or networking, I was fortunate to be able to have long conversations with many of them. Even with their varied backgrounds, I have come to realize that most of these people share a common trait—pessimism. They are uncertain about their present and, to them, the future looks bleak. Most don't know what they want out of life. And those that do, set that notion aside, believing what they desire is unattainable.

Ami Ahuja is different. She has a happy, positive attitude about everything in life—even when she has had good reason not to. Such as when helping her mother battle cancer on three separate occasions, or when we lost our brick-and-mortar retail business and went into debt for over $250K, or those times I (her husband) have wanted to start a new venture or implement a new idea. Ami has always supported me full force, never once complaining about anything.

Ami's positivity is infectious. She instills it on our children. She radiates it with her friends. She spreads it far and wide among the 880+ members of her women's group. In fact, no one has made a greater impact on improving the lives of these women than Ami.

Thanks to Ami for sharing her UMBRELLA—a figurative umbrella that shows you the way, step by step, to increasing positivity in your life, removing negativity, and achieving goals. The UMBRELLA concepts are easy to understand, remember, and implement. I know, because Ami is living proof that her UMBRELLA steps work.

Would you like to see your life through a new set of eyes? You can, with U-M-B-R-E-L-L-A. In fact, many of these concepts can be implemented immediately, so you will experience change in a matter of days, not weeks or months.

Enough from me. Get on with reading the book. I know just how infectious Ami's enthusiasm is, and I hope you catch a good dose of it! Read the book with an open mind; put the concepts to use in your everyday life; and watch as the life you've always dreamed about becomes reality.

Sonny Ahuja
Helping Entrepreneurs KiLLitOnLine
www.SonnyAhuja.com

Introduction

Umbrella: Something which provides protection; something which covers or embraces a broad range of elements or factors (according to Merriam-Webster).

An umbrella serves literally as a shield that guards us from the elements—from drenching rains and from harsh, direct rays of sun. In this case, the elements cause physical harm and damage, some of which may be permanent.

Recently, I looked over the course of my own life—at the challenges and experiences I've faced—and come up with a more figurative definition and use of the word *umbrella*. My umbrella safeguards and defends against negativity (that is, against the harsh elements life sometimes serves us) while simultaneously offering protection and safety.

When we feel protected and safe for a period of time, whether it is for five minutes, five hours, five days, or longer, we cannot help but feel a growing sense of certainty and confidence. In fact, regardless of the type or duration of negativity we may have experienced previously (or continue to experience), our umbrella is most useful in serving to give us an overall increased sense of positivity.

Throughout our lives, we will continue to experience destructive and discouraging actions, words, thoughts, and deeds. While we might prefer to be completely shielded from this negativity, reason tells us this is not possible. What is possible, however, is to find a good source of strength and support for dealing with harmful behaviors.

To that end, we all need an umbrella of our own. What follows is your figurative umbrella, with each letter of the word—*u-m-b-r-e-l-l-a*—providing the wisdom and guidance you need to being, and remaining, positive in the midst of the darkest storm.

U
Understand

The first letter in the word *umbrella* is the letter *U*. In our figurative umbrella of positivity and wisdom, U stands for *Understand*.

Understand: to grasp the meaning of. Synonymous with: comprehend; recognize; realize; identify, know, appreciate.

Understand Yourself

First and foremost, you must understand yourself; you must understand who you are in general. Are you a positive person? Are you a negative person carrying around destructive thoughts in your head? If you can honestly recognize and admit you are a negative person, you are on your way to being able to remove the blockage of negativity.

> *You must be the change you wish to see in the world.*
> *~ Mahatma Gandhi*

Think of a grease or hair blockage in a pipe. Clean, fresh water is unable to flow freely because something is blocking its path and stopping it from moving forward. In that same way, if you get angry at something or someone, that anger blocks the flow of productive communication and satisfying outcomes.

If something angers you, sit down and ask yourself why. You need to understand exactly what angers you. For example, are you upset because you're sick? Are you mad because you don't have money to buy everything you want? Are you irritated because you find yourself attracted to someone you know is not right for you? Answer honestly.

When you honestly admit your anger, you can more readily realize and accept that sometimes things are the way they are just because: because some people are more prone to illness than others; because there will always be people with more money than you have; because when we're in love (or think we're in love), it's easy to overlook the other person's faults.

> *You cannot climb the ladder of success dressed in the costume of failure.*
> ~ *Zig Ziglar*

Realize, too, that we don't have control over many of life's happenings. The flip side to that realization is that there are just as many things, if not more, over which we can—and do—exercise control. So, rather than fume and lose sleep over those things that are out of your hands, understand them and you will be on your way to understanding yourself.

Always remember, the most difficult times in your life do not occur when no one understands you (or you think they don't understand you). The most difficult time is when you don't understand yourself, because that is when you can get yourself in a lot of trouble. Learn and study yourself. I cannot stress how important that is. Don't waste time and energy studying others. You can't control them. You can only control yourself, your emotions, your decisions.

Get on it now. Understand yourself and you'll be much better positioned to reducing, if not eliminating, the unproductive and unsatisfying blockages in your life, and opening the way to positivity and happiness.

Understand Your Needs

Everyone should know what they need and want out of life. Understanding your own needs is critically important, as that awareness drives many of the decisions you make in life. Understanding your own needs and wants also contributes to what you perceive as your success (or failure) in life.

Understand

When I talk about needs, I'm not referring to needing orange juice for breakfast or needing a new pair of shoes. The needs I'm concerned with in this book are your life's larger needs:

- What do you need so you feel you have the very best life possible?
- What do you need in terms of a job that will make you happy? Do you need a job that satisfies strictly your most basic requirements for food and shelter, or do you need a job that allows you to live a particular lifestyle?
- What do you need or want in terms of a husband or life partner?

Bear in mind, when determining and defining your needs, do not let them define you. More importantly, do not rely on them for your ultimate happiness or success. If you do, you are setting yourself up for disappointment. What happens should you fail to attain them?

So, find out what you really need, what you really want. The exercise won't be in vain. Why? Because once you know and recognize what you need and want, you are well positioned to either go and get it or ask for it! (How else would you expect to achieve your needs?)

What happens if you don't define your needs and wants? The worst case scenario is that you'll never get what you want out of life—ever. The next worse scenario is that your needs are fulfilled either incorrectly or only partially. You'll be confused and look in the wrong direction or seek assistance from people who really have no clue as to how to help.

In 2008, when the U.S. economy took a huge downturn, my own financial situation (and that of my husband and family) suffered as well. Our businesses failed, and we ended up with significant debt. I felt very much the victim, and shed quite a few tears over the unfortunate hand we had been dealt. I hadn't asked for those troubles and felt utterly confused, unsure of where to turn for help or what to do next.

I realized, quickly enough, that I had to do something. I took pen to paper and listed out my immediate needs. I listed my wants. I did some research and further defined and clarified my needs to determine the necessary steps to attain them. Only after understanding these essentials was I able to ask for suitable help or seek it out myself.

Did I lose time and money in the entire process of discovering my true wants and needs? Yes, you bet I did. But my desire is to help you work through this important step here and now so you don't waste another minute or spend another dime unnecessarily.

When you take the time to clearly determine and define your needs and wants, you'll know exactly what to ask for, and be that much closer to achieving everything you want out of life.

Understand the Uniqueness of Others

We are all different. We are all unique. We all think differently, have different desires, different ambitions—none of them better or worse than anyone else's—and all of them valid. The sooner you understand and accept everyone's uniqueness, the sooner you will be able to change your thought processes in terms of how you approach others.

If you don't acknowledge another person's differences, how can you expect to interact with that person appropriately? Full understanding and acceptance of everyone's differences means you will not misjudge others or treat them improperly. You must not judge or make assumptions based on incomplete knowledge or misperceptions.

Imagine you are having lunch at the cafeteria in your work place. You hear a woman at the next table talking in a loud, aggravating voice. You immediately conclude that, based on her outward behaviors, she is a negative or annoying person. While she may be, let's consider it from her perspective. We know she cannot change the voice she was

Understand

born with, so her voice is her voice. We don't know, however, if she has a hearing problem. Perhaps she is unable to hear the others at her table and, as usually, happens, talks in a loud enough voice that she can hear herself. Or, perhaps it is you who is sensitive to the tone and volume of her voice. Do you see how this works?

Every situation and scenario has multiple perspectives. There are two sides—maybe more—to every story. Learn and accept this. Better yet, tap into it and enjoy it. Remember, five fingers alone are never the same; each looks and feels different. But when they come together, they make a strong, powerful fist. When you appreciate everyone's uniqueness and individualism, you learn and you grow.

U is for *understand*. The **more you practice** the guidance outlined in this chapter, the easier it becomes to understand yourself, your needs, and the individuality of others. Use this wisdom to resolve an issue you may have with a co-worker, friend, or spouse, and you will release the negative energy that has been weighing you down. What could be more helpful than increasing the positivity in your world?

M
Manage

The second letter in the word *umbrella* is the letter *M*. In our figurative umbrella of positivity and wisdom, M stands for *Manage*.

Manage: to handle or direct with a degree of skill. Synonymous with: administer, supervise, control, handle.

When we think of the verb *to manage*, we often think of it in terms of managing a business. Let's take that understanding a step further, and consider it in terms of managing the business of *us*, of ourselves. We can easily recognize that, if we don't (that is, manage ourselves), things—us, our perspective, our world—get jumbled up, or worse, lost entirely.

Looking back, I recall the times I was lost. I was lost because I never managed. As a result, my life was lacking in those things that mattered to me at the time. Rather than be a victim of my own circumstances, I learned to manage—manage my time, my money, and my stress—and in time, my life changed for the better. Today, I am a successful entrepreneur; I have children—four loving children—and I have the best husband in the world. I became the manager of me, and now have everything I need and want out of life.

Manage Your Time

We are all familiar with the most typical time management techniques of making and prioritizing to-do lists, noting appointments and events on a calendar, and outlining a schedule every day. Books have been written on the subject of time management, and countless courses presented on the topic to individuals, executives, and professionals across the country. And I,

Manage

too, could fill this book with dozens of other time management tips and tricks for you, but I won't.

It's easy to buy into all that advice and wisdom. It all makes sense, right? In fact, you've probably even attempted to follow one or more nuggets of time-management guidance for a time. I bet, however, that after a week (or maybe even a month) you gave up. That's because, in order to manage your time, you have to, well, manage your time. Day in and day out, you have to be committed to following through on the techniques you learned and, ironically, that takes time. For many, it's just easier to fall back into the same old routine.

If that "same old, same old" wasn't working before, it's not going to work now. You can, however, make great strides in better managing your time once you identify your time vampires—those activities and people who suck the precious time out of your day. Time vampires take you away from more meaningful or higher priority activities and events, the ones intended to lead you to the things you most want out of life.

A time vampire could be an unexpected phone call from your mother, who's "just calling to see how the kids are doing." You wouldn't dare hang up on your mother. Or, would you? You can—trust me. You tell her it's not a good time to talk and that you'll call her back after you're done work (or exercise, or paying bills, or writing in your journal...). Your mother, or whoever called, will certainly understand. If she doesn't, you need to address that with her separately.

Every person on this planet has 24 hours in their day. I have 24 hours. You have 24 hours. Bill Gates has 24 hours. It is, however, what you do in those 24 hours that can make or break you. How you manage each 24-hour allotment can mean the difference between success and failure, or success and constant struggle, or success and missed opportunity.

One easy way to better manage your time on a daily basis is to address your time vampires. Take an honest look at those habits that waste more of your time than you care to admit, and change or eliminate them. One culprit is email. If you are like me, you probably receive an excess of what can easily be labeled as junk email. You know it's junk email, but the subject line is so interesting, you just have to open the message, and then, of course, read through the catchy text, and look at the pretty images and photos, and click on the link that takes you to a multi-page website, and maybe do some shopping... And there you have it. You've fallen into the trap, and in the process lost precious time. I used to do that.

Social media, especially Facebook, is another time vampire, maybe even the worst. Some people spend hours—yes, hours—a day scrolling through their newsfeed to see who's posted what; who's said what about their status; who's liked their comment, etc. Pinterest is another trap. You're going to log on quickly because you just need an idea to decorate for a child's birthday party. You end up looking at dozens (hundreds?) of pictures of all types of parties and events, of all themes and for all ages.

Why do we behave this way with social media? Because it's fun; it really is. We are only human, and we are curious about so much. But we need to be disciplined in the amount of time we spend on these sites. Log in, give yourself a few minutes to look around and make a comment or two, and then log out. Know when it's time to switch gears and move on to the next activity—theoretically the one that is higher priority and taking you in the direction of your life's goals.

I learned to be disciplined about my Facebook usage from Perry Marshall, entrepreneur, online marketing strategist, and author. He, too, was a Facebook junkie, going back and forth between his work and checking Facebook all day. He finally got a handle on the constant checking by logging in to Facebook, allowing himself a brief period of time to be logged in, and then logging out of it completely. I now employ this tactic, and it works. You see, logging back in is an inconvenience; therefore, the simple step of staying logged out saves time and ultimately increases productivity. I've trained myself to only log into Facebook at a set time, and also to spend no more time than is absolutely necessary for what I want to do.

Surfing the net is another time waster. Who isn't tempted to pore through the Amazon, Kohl's, Target, or Macy's websites, trying to snag the best deal with percent-off or buy-one-get-one offers? The pictures and images are eye-catching and colorful, and they have so many options from which to choose, you can't help but scroll and scroll and scroll. Are you really getting a deal? I don't think so, because the truth is, these sites snagged you! And, they probably did so by sending you a junk email!

Unsubscribe to the junk and clutter, the emails, updates, and sales notices from marketers, and imagine the time—and money—you'll save. If you must, select one or two of the stores or companies with whom you do the most business to continue receiving their emails, but limit the number you receive from them. For example, rather than receiving daily emails, opt to receive them only weekly or when the vendor is having a special sales event.

Manage Your Money

Equally important as managing your time is managing your money. I touched on this in the previous section, but once you get a handle on your time vampires, you might also see positive results in terms of better management of your money.

Everyone knows the importance of proper money management. The bad news is that we live in a society of instant gratification. We see something we want, and we want it *now*. So we buy it now. Think of the stereotype of the woman who absolutely *has* to have—today— the newest fashion in shoes. (This stereotype formed for good reason.)

Or we've developed a habit that gives little to no return on our financial investment, for example, the daily Starbucks Iced Caramel Macchiato. The money you pay for this so-called "treat" is draining your wallet. This becomes clear when you do the math. According to FastFoodMenuPrices.com, the average price for the smallest size, ironically called *tall*, is $3.65. If you buy this drink five times a week, you're paying $18.25 every week, which multiplies to over $73 a month. Let me repeat: $73 every month. That's nearly $900 a year!

Now, we call this drink a treat because we feel we've earned it, we deserve it because we've had a stressful day, we took a 20-minute walk, our boss is mean—or because of any other countless excuses we choose to serve up. In actuality, a treat should be considered a luxury, an indulgence, something special to be enjoyed occasionally. In this case, our "treat" is not a compulsory daily sugar fix that damages not only what could and should be a sound savings plan, but also our waistline.

When some people hear the words *money management*, they feel they have to cut back on so many things and drastically change the way they live. To the contrary, the ultimate objective of proper money management is to be able to live life to the fullest. After all, we only live once. And while it may sound counterintuitive, the best way to live life to the fullest is to spend less money and invest more of it. It is only through sound saving and investing strategies that you will be able to grow and multiply your personal wealth.

There are several steps you can take to hone your money management skills. One is to seek the advice of a financial advisor. Educate yourself on financial terminology and the most common strategies, including learning the best ways to invest that extra $900 you'll have each year when you stop paying for specialty coffee drinks. Attend a consultation, which, often times, are free. In some cases, you might even be able to attend as part of a group presentation that includes dinner—a free meal is always a good start to saving money!

While you're waiting for your appointment with a financial advisor, be proactive about investing and managing money. Take time to research topics that interest you. For example, if you are interested in the medical or legal professions, buy a book on the topic, research it on the Internet, or seek a mentor in the field. If your place of employment offers tuition reimbursement, take advantage of that benefit to enroll in a class or degree program to learn new skills. Time and money spent on resources to educate yourself about a particular area of interest are both worthwhile investments. And, logically, the more knowledgeable and expert you become on a topic, the more marketable you become—something that will give an excellent return on that initial investment.

Consider your life goals, including short- and long-term goals. What do you want most out of life that requires money? Do you want to be able to buy a new car every four years? Do you want to save for your children's college education? Do you dream of owning a second home at the beach? Once you've identified your goals and implemented a plan for saving money and managing your finances, your entire thought process about money will change. The next time you're tempted to buy a new purse, you'll find yourself asking, "Do I really need this?" If the answer is no, don't buy it. Put the money you would have spent on the purse into your savings account and watch it grow.

When you learn how to manage your money and take steps to save and invest, you'll realize you are on track to meeting your weekly, monthly, and yearly financial goals, and you'll feel a tremendous sense of satisfaction and accomplishment as you watch things come together.

Remember, too, that success comes in all sizes. You do not achieve success only at the moment in time when you buy a new car. Consider the steps you followed to get to that point:

1. You enrolled in a Marketing certification course through your employer.
2. You completed the course and turned in proof of satisfactory completion.
3. Your employer reimbursed you for the cost of tuition for the course.
4. You gained wisdom and confidence from having completed the course, and with this new-found knowledge, applied for a job in your company's marketing department.

5. You got the job, which is a promotion in both title and salary.
6. You implemented proper money management skills and saved enough money from your improved pay to make a sizeable down payment on a car.
7. You enjoyed the oohs and aahs of your friends and co-workers when you pulled into the parking lot at work behind the wheel of your new car.

Items one through six on the above list are all individual successes on the way to the larger success of buying a new car. Look at the actions you took along the way. Find clues and commonalities in them that can be repeated as you work to achieve your next goal, your next success. This includes, of course, implementing appropriate time and money management skills.

Manage Your Stress

Stress is our emotional and/or physical reaction or response to stressors or stimuli in our environment, whether at work or at home. Everyone experiences stress to one degree or another, and at one time or another. Even yoga-exercising/chai-tea-drinking/meditation-practicing people experience stress on occasion.

According to the American Institute of Stress (AIS), numerous emotional and physical disorders have been linked to stress, which affects our mood and behavior. Physiologically, stress also affects the various systems, organs, and tissues of our body, and can lead to disease and disorders such as depression and anxiety, heart attacks and stroke, disturbances of our immune system and increased susceptibility to illness and infection. Stress can also impact relationships both at home and at work. In fact, couples often cite stress from one factor or another as a main cause of their problems and discord.

The demands of day-to-day living, our jobs, our kids, our parents, all cause stress. You will probably agree that the most typical and significant stressors are money problems—we never seem to have enough, and time—there are never enough hours in the day.

Manage

Stress is unhealthy, and very serious stuff. It is not to be taken lightly. It must be managed, and managed in a way that gets you the best results. Recognize when you need a break, a time away, and take action. Don't wait for someone to suggest you go shopping or to bring you beautiful flowers to look at and smell. That suggestion may never come. For your own health, and the health of your relationships, take the time to take care of yourself.

Different people relieve their stress different ways. Some women relieve stress by going shopping—because they had a bad day and feel they deserve to get something nice for themselves. Other women turn to food and drink—ice cream, potato chips, wine—as a way to relieve their stress and "nurture" their hurting minds and bodies. Spending money and eating or drinking to excess are not stress relievers. They are stress inducers.

If you go shopping when you are stressed, you are likely to spend more money than you should or spend money on things you don't need. You know you should be saving rather than spending, and as a result, end up more stressed than you were before going shopping. If you grab a carton of ice cream or bottle of wine when you're stressed, you're liable to eat the entire container or drink the entire bottle, and feel guilty afterward for having done so. You'll worry about gaining weight or having a hangover, and ultimately be even more stressed out than you were before eating or drinking a thing.

When deciding on what works best for you in terms of how to reduce stress, even temporarily, the key is to *do something that gives you a break from your normal daily routine*. Healthy stress relievers include exercise such as running, yoga, or walking. If you enjoy being in the company of others, go out with friends for a dinner or to the movies, or organize a girls' night in. If you prefer solitude and quiet, escape with that book you've been putting off starting or do what I do—take a long, hot shower, long enough that the hot water tank empties. Laughter is known to be an excellent form of stress relief. Watch a comedy show on TV or rent a long-time favorite comedy movie.

M is for *manage*. Properly done, management eliminates chaos and uncertainty, and results in organization and order—and ultimately, success. Remember, you can be successful many times over. When you achieve success, no matter how small, go back, find the clue to what you did, and repeat it for continued success. Speaking from experience, I can say the clues are not always obvious. You sometimes have to dig deep to find them. But the result you'll achieve will be worth it. I've mastered a few skills in life, both personal and professional, and been enjoying repeated success for over five years. At this point, I don't ever have to look back. That feeling is awesome.

B
Build

The third letter in the word *umbrella* is the letter *B*. In our figurative umbrella of positivity and wisdom, B stands for *Build*.

Build: to form by ordering and uniting materials by gradual means into a composite whole.

This definition of the word *build* implies there is to be a proper and logical progression to reach the finished product and desired results.

Consider how a house is built. The basic requirement for any building to be structurally sound and safe is to ensure the foundation on which it is built is strong and solid. Without an adequate foundation, the building could fall and crumble—and the entire structure would be destroyed.

Equally important are the walls, the ceilings, the roof, and the windows. We then need plumbing and electricity. From there we progress to the finer details that result in this structure becoming a home—your home—where you feel safe and comfortable, and are surrounded by the things you cherish, those personal belongings that have meaning to you.

Consider now how you build everything else in life, figuratively and literally. The process is the same. Start with a solid foundation, and gradually add to it by ordering and uniting the necessary components until you have a finished product.

Build Relationships

Countless books have been written on personal relationships—starting them, growing them, developing them—but the relationship-building topic I touch on here addresses professional relationships (personal relationship-building is a topic for an entirely different book). Professional relationships are critical if you want to succeed in your chosen line of work. When you foster these relationships and convert them from the cordial "It's-a-pleasure-to-meet-you" type to the "Congratulations-on-the-big-sale" type, you take yourself up one rung on your own ladder to success.

This conversion doesn't happen overnight or by seeing a person just one time. Relationships take time to grow and flourish. Sound like work? It is, but it is fun, interesting work. And if this work does nothing more than bring one new friend into your life, it will have been worth the effort.

What is the best way to build new professional relationships from the ground up? Quite simply, tried and true networking. Start with like-minded groups or businesses that fit your target base of potential customers. Attend presentations and networking events where you're sure to meet new people and start new relationships. You will all have something in common, and that is always a great conversation opener. Once you discover your commonalities, you'll have enough information to be able to further nourish the relationship and keep it growing.

Networking has tremendous potential. Get as much out of it as you can. And don't be afraid to go it alone. I've attended many events alone and, while it might be a bit uncomfortable at first, as soon as I remind myself that I'm not the only person in the room by myself and also that everyone is there for the same purpose, I easily shake off my nerves and get right to work.

And, when you attend events alone, others view you as more approachable than if you are with another woman attached to you at the hip the entire time. Networking should be a positive event, and you will probably learn something new at each event you attend.

Look at it this way: When you attend a networking event, you build new relationships. When you build new relationships, you get new clients. New clients means your business grows, which leads to success, and further success—all a positive flow, and all the logical progression you need to follow to reach your finished product and desired results. Once you've established this positive flow of relationships, good things will happen.

Build a Magnetic Personality

Do you know anyone with a magnetic personality, someone you are drawn to for their positive qualities and optimistic attitude? Maybe you've never thought of their personality as magnetic, or even pinpointed the person's characteristics and qualities, but you know you like them, you like talking to them, and you enjoy being in their company.

Do you have a magnetic personality? I bet most of you reading this right now probably shrugged your shoulders, shook your head, and answered "I don't know" or "Not exactly" or "Some people tell me I do."

Do *you* think you have a magnetic personality? Your answer to this question might be more like "I might," "I think I do," or "How can I tell?"

> The starting point of all achievement is desire.
> ~ Napoleon Hill

Do you detect in any of these answers a lack of self-confidence and even, perhaps, some self-deprecation? The truth is, the person with a magnetic personality has self-confidence. That person would have answered the first question with an energetic "Yes," and the second question with and equally energetic "Yes"—nothing wishy-washy there. And they would have done so in their own authentic style. So, be yourself, and be confident in who you are, what you do, and what you say.

People with a magnetic personality also know their stuff. They know what's going on locally and globally, so they can contribute to conversations. They know what's going on in their own business environment and area of expertise, so they can promote and motivate. When you are truly knowledgeable on a topic and can speak clearly, concisely, and thoughtfully on it, people view you as an authority on the subject, and will naturally be drawn to you for information and possible even advice. This is powerful, as the side benefit is that you will also be viewed as motivational and capable of inspiring others.

Just as we are easily attracted to people with a magnetic personality, we are easily put off by negative people. We tend to avoid those who are constantly critical of their situation, their lot in life, the people around them. Pessimism is not an alluring quality. The bottom line is that like attracts like. We've all heard the saying that misery loves company. But, it's much more fun to be optimistic and positive than it is to be Debbie Downer or have to support her and build her up all the time.

> *Try to be a rainbow in someone's cloud.*
> *~ Maya Angelou*

If you are energetic and upbeat, you will find fun and humor in any situation and help others do the same. If you speak meaningfully and authentically, people will listen; they will consider you honest and credible, and want to do business with you or be part of whatever you're involved in.

Embrace the qualities of people you believe have magnetic personalities. Don't imitate or try to be exactly like them, as others will pick up on your phoniness. When you are yourself and you come across as genuine, people will naturally respect and love you.

Build a Legacy

Have you ever thought about building or leaving a legacy? When people hear the word *legacy*, most think of what they plan to leave to their children or family when they die. To them, a legacy is something to eventually be passed down—money, a piece of land or other property, a stamp collection, or some item of sentimental value. Their legacy is usually spelled out in their last will and testament.

I agree that having a will is important to ensure your assets are appropriately managed and disbursed, and that your final wishes are carried out. How else would your legacy survive into the future?

I also believe it's possible to work on setting up your legacy now—today. Why not make a difference in the here and present? Why not work on your legacy while you are still here to experience and enjoy the fruits of its results? Done right, the difference you make today will last for generations.

A good way to start work on building your legacy is to be a role model to your friends and family. Set an example others will want to follow. We all know just how smart children are. They watch your every move. They pick up on your words. They are anxious to copy you and follow in your footsteps—and they often do. Who hasn't been embarrassed when, at the least appropriate moment, their child says a naughty word they heard another adult use?

Live your life—walk and talk—in a way that sets the tone for the legacy you want to convey. When my youngest daughter was 3, I observed her one time pretending to be me. She was talking on the phone and playacting that she was taking perfume orders, something she'd seen me do countless times. At the end of her call, she even told me she had made $300!

Now, I'm not going to put my daughter to work supporting our family, but she has learned that her mother takes a proactive role in her work and is successful at the job she does. The legacy I'm building here is the positive message of self-help I gave my daughter.

B is for *Build*. When you build or construct something—a building, a relationship, a business—always start with a solid foundation and build up from there. Along the way, countless other opportunities to build something of value will present themselves. Take advantage of all that you can, and you'll be well on your way to building your success.

R
Remove

The fourth letter in the word *umbrella* is the letter *R*. In our figurative umbrella of positivity and wisdom, R stands for *Remove*.

Remove: to change the location, position, station, or residence of.

I would take this definition of the word *remove* a step further to add that it implies extraction, that is, a move—or removal—by force. When you need to remove something, or move it forcibly, you take a conscious action to change its location.

Why remove? We might remove things—items or people, including ourselves—from their present location because they are needed elsewhere, they are causing harm or damage in their present location, we no longer need them, or they serve no useful purpose in their current position. Consider what you might remove from your own life, your own surroundings, that distracts you or gets in the way of your ability to meet your goals or achieve success.

Remove Negativity

We all have our ups and downs in life. We all have moments when we are sad or down or depressed. Those feelings are normal and, I would contend, also necessary for proper emotional health. The trouble occurs, however, when you—or someone you know—are in a negative state of mind all the time.

> *Positive thinking will let you do everything better than negative thinking will.*
>
> ~ *Zig Ziglar*

Constant negativity is an emotional drain. We all know someone who is chronically pessimistic about every situation in life, who does nothing but complain about others, about their lot in life, about everything. It quickly becomes exhausting to have to listen to this person and have to constantly *try* to build them up and reassure them that everything will be all right. After a while, you recognize that nothing you say or do will alter that person's thinking or state of mind. When you reach that point, it's time to move on. And if, after reading this, you realize there are people in your life who fit the negativity old, I advise you to ditch them now. Sounds cruel, no? Trust me, it's not. You know you've tried to fix him or her, tried to bolster their ego, tried to tell them that their constant negativity is not healthy for anyone, and yet they don't change. So, yes, get rid of the negative people from your life as much as possible.

You have enough personal and professional issues to deal with that you don't need to be dragged down by someone else's. Your own sanity, peace of mind, and happiness are at stake. They are too valuable to risk losing, as you need these resources on your own path to success.

If you eliminate a negative person from your life, and that person questions the sudden distance between you and them, tell them the truth. Maybe your admission to them will trigger just the change in their behavior they need.

Remove the News

I don't watch the news on TV. We live in a world where bad things happen, and the news seems to report only on bad things. If you watch enough negative news stories, you can't help but get negative or depressed yourself.

That is not to say we should not stay informed on what's going on in the world. To the contrary, when you understand and are current on world events, you can be an intelligent contributor to a conversation.

One way to stay current is to look online. Go to your favorite news source and scroll through the headlines. That gives you very high-level information—information which, I should say, you should always take with a grain of salt. Don't be influenced or swayed by a single headline. If a particular topic, person, or situation catches your interest, dig deeper to learn more about what is being discussed, and form your own opinion on the matter.

But, remove the most negative of the news flashes and headlines from your life. Bad things happen, and we can be grateful they aren't happening to us. We can wish others the will and strength to get through their negative situations, and then move on. That, in itself, takes strength on our part, as we are so used to being drawn in and swept away by the news, bad news in particular.

Remove Clutter

Clutter is a difficult topic to discuss. So many of us have "things" we don't ever want to get rid of, but if we are honest with ourselves, those things are, in fact, clutter. And clutter means disorder, confusion, interference, and lack of organization.

But, you say, "I'm keeping this because one day I'll need it." And so, your closets, drawers, basement, and attic get filled with things you think you'll need one day. Baloney! "One day" never comes. You never need whatever it was that you so carefully tucked away on the shelf in the far corner of the storage room in your basement. Chances are, you don't even remember what's in all that clutter.

Again you say, "I'm keeping this because my husband gave it to me for my birthday." Really? Which birthday/anniversary/Valentine's Day? If you don't know, and you haven't used, read, worn, looked at, or eaten whatever that precious gift was in more than a few months, you don't need it. I say to all of you sentimental ladies out there, your husband is your biggest gift, the best present you'll ever need.

Get rid of clutter, wherever it resides—your living room, bathroom vanity, office, even that catch-all drawer in the kitchen. Have a garage sale or donate your items to charity, to Habitat for Humanity, to a women's shelter, to the SPCA.

Clutter is just one big blockage, both literally and figuratively. It tells the universe you are full and that you don't need anything at all.

When you have clutter, you stop receiving new, good stuff—the stuff that really matters in life.

Clutter and the blockage it represents prevent your inner voice and thoughts from being delivered because you can't see or think beyond everything that's crowding your life. When that happens, how can you possibly expect to obtain or receive what you really desire or need to succeed?

You'll find that, when you eliminate the clutter and the blockage, your thought patterns change. You see things more clearly and in a more orderly fashion. From there, you begin to transmit the correct signal, and open yourself up to receiving so much more of what you really desire out of life.

Remove Evil Thoughts

I want to say that evil thoughts should be a very easy thing to remove from our lives. I also recognize that sometimes, in anger, our thoughts and emotions rage out of control.

Perhaps you've been slighted, or lied to, or cheated out of something of value, or hurt in some other unthinkable way. Horrible, revenge-filled thoughts fill your head: "I hate her—I wish she were dead" or "I hope his new girlfriend dumps him like a hot potato, just like he dumped me" or "What an idiot—he doesn't know a thing about this problem."

> *An eye for an eye only ends up making the whole world blind.*
> *~ Mahatma Gandhi*

These are evil thoughts, and you need to get rid of them. They hurt no one but you, as they fester and build and add to your hurt, anger, and frustration. It helps to remember what goes around, comes around. How many times have you been out driving and suddenly another driver cuts you off? Your first inclination might be to make an obscene gesture or tailgate—neither of which is a good option. Just relax, ease off on the gas pedal, and watch what happens. Sure enough, another driver will eventually do the exact same thing to him

Remove

or her. Justice will have been served, and your blood pressure will not have taken any hits.

It takes all kinds of people to make the world go around. We don't have to like them all. We don't have to agree with them all. But we do have to live with them, and they with us. If you don't like a particular person, that's fine. Just move on and be happy in your own world. Don't waste your time thinking evil thoughts. It is unproductive, and again, the only one who suffers is you. Fix and train your thoughts to be directed away from the person or situation that upsets you, and more positively focused.

The same holds true for someone who has evil or negative thoughts about you, someone who is part of your home or work life. I hope this never happens, but if it does, realize that people have different opinions and thoughts about you, your family, your home, your job, your children, your friends, etc. Remind yourself that there are always at least two sides to every story, and multiple perspectives when viewing a painting or photo.

As long as you rid yourself of evil thoughts, and set the example to others who do have such negative thought processes, you are headed in the right direction. Don't let bad thoughts—yours or theirs—drain you.

R is for *Remove*. When you remove negativity, clutter, and evil thoughts from your life, you will have lifted a cloud of darkness and oppression from overhead. You will have removed whatever it was that was blocking you from being successful, and enabled your ability to enjoy the moment, the present.

I always enjoy every moment of my life. I enjoy every second of my life. I enjoy every second of my sleep. My husband Sonny tells me that when he wakes up in the middle of the night and looks at me, he sees me smiling in my sleep, smiling from contentedness. Why? Because I trained my thoughts to be positive and happy all the time.

8 Easy Ways to Jump-Start Your Happiness

Everybody can do it. I am not Einstein. I am just normal. Anybody can do it. Honestly.

To learn more on this topic, visit www.AmiAhuja.com to download your free copy of "7 Ways to Remove Negativity."

E
Empower

The fifth letter in the word *umbrella* is the letter *E*. In our figurative umbrella of positivity and wisdom, E stands for *Empower*.

Empower: to give official authority or legal power to.

My dictionary provides another definition of the word *empower*: enable.

Our use of the word *enable*, or any of its other forms, such as *enabler*, can connote something either positive or negative. Consider these:

- Amanda's raise in salary enabled her to save more money each month toward the down payment on her next car.
- Madeline enabled her husband to continue his habit of leaving his dirty laundry on the floor by picking it up and putting it in the laundry hamper every morning.

The use of *enabled* in the first sentence clearly has a positive connotation because the end result of Amanda's raise is a positive, constructive action: saving more money, which ultimately leads to Amanda being able to buy a car.

The use of *enabled* in the second sentence has a negative connotation in that Madeline lets her husband get away without taking responsibility for his own dirty laundry. We could carry the negative effects of this story even further when we think that Madeline has to drop what she's doing to pick up her husband's dirty clothes; she's is tired of telling her husband to clean up after himself; and she gets frustrated because her husband is a slob, etc. etc.

Now substitute the word *empowered* for *enabled* in both sentences. The substitution works in the first example, as Madeline, with her new and improved salary, feels empowered to do even more for herself and, so, saves more money. The substitution does not work in the second sentence. Why? Because the connotation in the original sentence is negative. Madeline would certainly not empower her husband to continue a habit that is so bad for their marriage.

The takeaway is that, when we empower others or feel empowered ourselves, it is generally for the greater good—personally, professionally, individually, or as a group.

Empowering Characteristics

The empowered woman possesses certain characteristics and qualities that define her as empowered. She's not naturally born with them as she would be born with brown eyes or black hair. She must learn these traits, develop them and cultivate them over time, based on her life's education, experiences, opportunities, and decisions—and especially, her inner strength.

What the Empowered Woman Is *Not*:

Just to clear the air and dispel any misperceptions you may have, let us first consider those characteristics that do *not* define an empowered woman. Empowered does not mean pushy, aggressive, loud, or overbearing. It does not mean rude, disrespectful, or inconsiderate. Empowered does not disallow, reject, disenfranchise, or disapprove.

If your husband, boyfriend, significant other, father, son or any other male in your life uses any of the words in the preceding paragraph in their own definition of empowered, smile sweetly and hand them this list. In other words, feel empowered to educate them otherwise.

What the Empowered Woman Is:

As an empowered woman, you are accountable to yourself. You know who you are and what you want. You might not know *how* to get it, but you have the wherewithal to figure it out. Or, you might need help to get what you want, but you are not afraid to ask for whatever help you need.

When you are empowered, you are constantly in search of ways to do what you want, so that you can live your dream and your passions at every moment. You shun the people, jobs, activities, and events that take you in the opposite direction. And, while others may try to trip you up along the way or make you feel guilty for constantly acting on your dreams, you deal with this negativity in a positive manner because you know your passions are worthy goals and the best gifts you can give yourself and others.

If you are empowered, you understand the key to your relationships, both personal and professional, is to enter and remain in only those that enhance your ability to meet your goals and follow your passion. If it means changing jobs or removing negative or contrary people from your life, if you are truly empowered, you will do it. That is not to say it will be easy, but when you realize your growth potential without having those contrary relationships in your life, taking that leap doesn't seem that bad.

The empowered woman possesses many other wonderful, beautiful qualities. I mention the most noteworthy here, because they are what you need to get started—in the event you are teetering on the edge between full empowerment and accepting the challenge to proceed with your dreams—and to help you keep the feelings of empowerment strong within.

Empower Others

I receive joy and happiness out of empowering others. That's because, when you empower others, you bring positivity upon yourself. One thing that is difficult for me, personally, to understand, is that some women actually hold off on empowering other women because they are jealous of the potential success of these other women. This confuses me, and I don't understand why.

Each of us, with our own unique beauty, qualities, personalities, skills, and experience(s) are empowered to succeed and shine in our own light, in our own right. The overlap is our gender only. There truly is enough room on the planet for all empowered women to co-exist. When we help, encourage, and empower others, we are helping, encouraging, and empowering ourselves.

A sign as simple as a smile is contagious. When you smile at someone, they smile back, no matter how busy or in a rush they are. That one act of me smiling at one person, and that one person smiling back is uplifting—for both of us. I know I am already energized and ready to encourage others, and maybe, just maybe, I brought energy and encouragement to that other person. What an amazingly powerful result.

In what other ways can we empower others? We can sit with them, talk with them, listen to them, help them. I know, I know, we're all busy and barely have time to take care of ourselves let alone someone else who needs support. I can honestly say that the return on your investment of even a few minutes of time spent empowering someone else is tremendous. You will have invested not only in helping that person's emotional/mental/financial/physical success, but in your own as well. You cannot help but reap similar benefits by helping others.

> *We can't help everyone, but everyone can help someone.*
> *~ Ronald Reagan*

Empowering others often entails providing opportunities for networking and connecting. When you connect two people with common interests and values, the foundation is already in place for a new friendship to form. (Remember the *B* in *Build*?) That connection of like-minded women will take them far. If they nurture their relationship, they will experience—together and individually—new, different, and exciting things.

Remember, by empowering others, you also nurture and empower yourself.

Empower Yourself

The last sentence of the previous section bears repeating: By empowering others, you also nurture and empower yourself. This is, perhaps, the best first step toward empowering yourself. Even if today you may not be feeling especially empowered (although I don't know why, with all those smiles you're giving out), when you have invested the time in supporting another woman, you get your own dose of positive energy in return. It really is that simple.

Another step to take on your path to empowerment is to network. Networking is not just for professionals in the workplace to attend Chamber of Commerce events to meet other professionals. Think of the word *network* in the broadest of senses, and put its power to work for you. When you network, you get out and meet others. You smile and shake hands. You share anecdotes and experiences. You expand your list of connections.

When you think about it, you can network just about any place—at book club, at the supermarket, at your kids' extracurricular activities, at girls' night out, at yoga class (before or after, of course!), at community gatherings, etc., etc. Hand out your card. If your current business or professional card is not appropriate, make a personal card to hand when an opportunity presents itself. This way, others will be encouraged to stay in touch with you. And likewise, get other people's phone and email address, and then use them. Stay in touch. Expand your relationships. This one minor step can lead to much bigger successes for you down the road.

Another way to empower yourself is through knowledge. We've all heard the expression Knowledge Is Power, so go for as much knowledge as you can. Gain book knowledge and hands-on experience on topics you love, topics that interest you, and topics that take you further down your path to success. Rack up classroom hours and volunteer time in your preferred activities.

How can you not feel empowered when you possess knowledge, intelligence, and expertise on a topic? And when you are informed, you feel more comfortable and confident in that knowledge, and will be better positioned to contribute to, or start, a conversation. You'll be encouraged to approach other experts, and people will view you as an expert and seek you out.

Are you starting to see how it all comes together? I don't know about you, but I'm feeling more empowered already!

E is for *Empower.* Other actions we take in the course of our daily routines lead to empowerment, even if our intent is not to directly empower. That's just one of the bonus benefits we reap.

For example, consider the coworker who earned the job promotion you were hoping to get—the job you prepared so hard for and waited so long for. Are you disappointed? Frustrated? Of course you are. Will you forever begrudge your coworker for beating you out of your dream job? I certainly hope not. You have several options on how you can proceed. 1) You can ignore your coworker and hope she fails in her new assignment; 2) You can congratulate her and wish her well; 3) You can learn what to improve on in order to be better prepared for the next opportunity.

Options 2 and 3 are the way to go. Option 2 keeps the work environment positive. You wouldn't want it any other way. And, you maintain your dignity and poise, which others will note and remember. Option 3 is your opportunity to gain knowledge—about yourself, your skills, your experience—so you know what to work on improving.

The decisions we make ultimately lead to us empowering ourselves and others. When you understand that, and the fact that you empower yourself each time you empower or encourage someone else, you quickly learn to make decisions that take you down that path.

> *Our greatest glory is not in never failing, but in rising up every time we fail.*
> *~ Ralph Waldo Emerson*

L
Listen

The sixth letter in the word *umbrella* is the letter *L*. In our figurative umbrella of positivity and wisdom, L stands for *Listen*.

Listen: to pay attention to sound; to hear something with thoughtful attention, as in give consideration.

I believe my Merriam-Webster's Collegiate Dictionary should change the order of the above definitions of the word *listen*. The first definition is so literal it immediately reminds me of the Peanuts™ character Charlie Brown sitting in his classroom at school, and listening to his teacher say "Wah wah wah wah wah wah wah wah" all day. He's paying attention, but what he hears is sound—white noise droning on and on. We never know if that sound has any sense or meaning to him, but I'd say it does not.

The second definition of the word *listen* is the one we should all live by. When we listen to someone or something, we should give it thoughtful attention, careful devotion, attentive regard. Otherwise, how would we know how to react or respond?

I recently saw a cartoon that said, "If a woman speaks and no one is listening, her name is probably Mom." That might be funny if it weren't so true. Mom's voice is that white noise that the children hear but tune out—until Mom's voice has to get louder or change tone to distract the children from whatever it is they're doing to actually pay attention.

Other huge distractions in today's world are cell phones and Facebook. We are all guilty of this. We rely on our phones to talk or text or email or post or follow, and we would do it 24/7 if we didn't have to sleep at some point. We connect with friends across the country and loved ones around the globe. Technology has made staying in touch easy. All good, no?

Sometimes yes; other times no. Often, we ignore the person seated across the table from us who's trying to have a conversation. In some cases, that person sits patiently waiting for us to finish whatever we're doing on our cell phone so as to have a conversation free of distraction and interruption. In other cases, that person continues to talk, and then asks a question, and then we say, "What? I'm sorry, what was that? I just had to get this picture posted on my Facebook page."

This scenario is not far from reality. In fact, I'm sure you can think of more than one instance where this has happened to you, too. Whether you're the one talking or the one with head bent and eyes glued to the phone. Some of us dismiss the behavior—probably because we're guilty of it or accept it as sign of the times—while others of us—myself included—find it unacceptable.

Think about it, the cell-phone user is not only *not* listening, he or she is disrespecting the other person, wasting their time, telling them they're not as important as the conversation taking place on the phone. When you go out for lunch or dinner with friends or your spouse, you are committing yourself to that relationship by giving an hour or two of your time. What if that lunch was with your boss, or a networking connection, or a mentor? What if they wanted to give you important news, confide in you, offer you a job?

When you leave your phone tucked away (that is, out of sight, not visible or audible), you show common courtesy and maturity. You are in the present. You are ready to give yourself to that person, and show them you respect and value them and their time as well. You are fully prepped and ready to really listen to what they have to say. You convey that they are important to you and that they have your undivided attention for a time. You actually empower them to speak.

Learn to Listen

The act of listening—*really* listening—has not always come easy to me. Just ask my husband. Maybe I was built that way. I have had to actually teach myself to listen. I've had to *learn to listen*. If you find it hard to listen to others, remember, it's not their fault; it means you have some other distraction going on. You need to learn to listen. Do that by eliminating the distraction, clearing your mind, and opening yourself to the other person. Practice. Listen with intention. The more you do this, the more you'll hear. The more you hear, the more you'll learn.

Maybe you don't like to listen because you don't like the person who is talking or you don't like the topic they're discussing or you think you have better things to do. If you have been placed in a situation, for example a mandatory meeting at work, accept that you are there and that you're there for a reason. If you are in church, but your mind wanders to the brunch you'll be attending afterwards, catch yourself and remember why you are there. Focus on the topic of the sermon with intent and really listen to the message. Practice and learn to listen.

Imagine all that results when you listen. You hear the other person's words and whatever message they want to convey. You may even find yourself hearing "hidden" words, that is, an even deeper meaning in what the other person is saying. What if they are asking for help, but not saying so in direct words? Through active listening, however, you probe and listen for more, and their message finally becomes clear. You are now in a position to respond appropriately by lending expertise and guidance to someone in need.

You will have helped another person, and maybe even solved a problem for them. Beyond that, you will have shown concern and respect, and added to the foundation of your relationship with them. Would you have been able to accomplish something so powerful if you'd been distracted by constant pings from your cell phone?

Another perspective of listening to someone is heeding what they say. So, yes, you hear their words, you hear what they're saying, but then you ignore it. Six years ago, my husband and I were setting up our online perfume business. Sonny told me to take pictures of our perfumes and upload them to our website. I didn't like the chore of taking the photos, uploading them, and arranging them on the website, so I didn't do it. I didn't listen to Sonny. I didn't heed his suggestion.

In time, I realized I was wrong, and ended up taking the pictures and getting them on the website. There's only so long I could have a notice on the website that said "Image coming soon." People want to see pictures of the products they are interested in buying. Attractive pictures make for an interesting website, which leads to more traffic on the website, and more business. By listening to Sonny, and following his advice, I solved a problem and reached a better solution. And, my success was two-fold: I didn't have to pay someone else to do this work and I improved my website and increased my profits.

It took practice, but I learned to listen and have enjoyed success as a direct result. Once you, too, master the art of listening by providing thoughtful attention, you will add to your own successes.

Listen to Children

Listen to what children have to say, whether they're your own children or someone else's. Children, in their innocence, teach us something every time we engage in conversation with them.

When you communicate with children you experience how they feel, how they view things, and how curious and interested they are in the world around them and beyond. The bonus to this is that a child's perspective on life and other people sparks something in you. It makes you think and want to dialogue with him or her. Don't miss the opportunity to make such a valuable connection.

Today, parents and children are busier than ever. There is always some chore to do at home or errand to run. Throw in a load of laundry, cook dinner, change the sheets on the bed, do the grocery shopping, and the list goes on. And, if both parents work outside the home, the list just got that much longer. Our tendency is to plop our children down in front of the TV or let them play a game on the computer or phone or other device, all so we can get our work done. And when children interrupt our phone conversation (or time on Facebook uploading a picture of them—how ironic!) we tell them we're busy and shoo them away. How sad for both of us—the parent and the child.

We will have missed an opportunity to listen, to nurture, to learn. What is more important than that when you're doing it with a child who has sought you out? Pay attention. Earn their trust. Build their confidence. Children will share their fears, hopes, and even secrets if your relationship is one of trust and open communication. When you listen to children, everyone benefits.

Listen to Colleagues and Coworkers

Listen to your coworkers. Don't report for work duty every day from nine to five and then hide in your cubicle the entire time. Your coworkers are you colleagues, maybe even your friends. Take time to cultivate or improve on your relationships with your coworkers.

In meetings, listen attentively to what they have to say. Before jumping in to either correct them or knock down their idea, acknowledge what they've said. This shows you've really heard them and respect them. A positive give-and-take of listening in the workplace lets people feel comfortable and confident in sharing their ideas and suggestions. You might even hear your coworker mention the next million-dollar idea!

In the cafeteria, listen to the lunchtime conversation and contribute. Make it a fun, social time. Seek colleagues who are positive and interesting. If the conversation is catty, move away from it. Don't waste your lunch break by being part of such negativity. If you have lunch with fun, friendly people, when you return to your desk afterwards, you are more upbeat yourself, and ready to face the afternoon.

L is for *Listen*. Listening is a two-way street. Just as we want others to listen to us when we speak (because what we have to say is very important), so should we listen with thoughtful attention when someone else speaks. Our magnetic personality shines through when we do that because the other person knows we are really listening and will want to open up to us. How powerful is that?

L
Learn

The seventh letter in the word *umbrella* is the letter *L*. In our figurative umbrella of positivity and wisdom, L stands for *Learn*.

Learn: to gain knowledge or understanding of, or skill in, by study, instruction, or experience.

I love to learn. Learning improves the health of my mind by exercising my brain muscles. Learning gives me new information and new insights every day. Learning tells me more about myself and others. What's not to love about learning? In this chapter, I share my insights into key aspects of life that go beyond learning book facts or multiplication tables.

Learn to Communicate

- "We don't see eye to eye."
- "We're just talking past each other."
- "You never pay attention to what I say."

Do any of these sound familiar? You may have said them yourself or perhaps had someone say them to you. To me, they are all the result of poor or lacking communications. Below are the respective reasons why each of the above statements would be said:

- You don't see eye to eye because you and the other person are not talking on the same level.
- You're talking past each other because you have different motives or objectives.
- The other person doesn't pay attention (or you think they don't pay attention) because, to them, you're speaking

gobbledegook (also known as jargon or in words that sound like a foreign language.)

All three problems have an easy solution. If you learn and practice the following tips, you will experience improvements in how you communicate with others and how others receive your message: Fix your communication style; adapt to the situation; be clear; be concise; know your audience and talk accordingly.

Also important is to communicate with an open mind. When your mind is open, you will be more accepting of the responses or reactions you'll receive from the other party, and everyone's stress level drops. You don't have to agree with them, and you don't have to like them, but you do have to listen to them, just as the other person listened to you. That's called two-way communication, and allows both parties the opportunity to present their view or position.

Note that I said two-way communication; I did not say three-way. Don't allow a third person to step into the communication stream. That will only muddy the waters, and leave one of the original two people feeling outnumbered, or worse, put them on the defensive.

Make sure your communications with your boss, your spouse, your clients are non-aggressive. When you communicate in an antagonistic or hostile manner, everything goes south. The recipient of your aggression will only tune you out, walk away, or return the favor with similar negativity, and then no one is happy, everyone is yelling, and nothing gets accomplished.

I'm a firm believer that you can deliver any kind of message you want, as long as you do it in the right way. Surely you've heard the expression "You can catch more flies with honey than with vinegar." This is so true, and a long time ago I learned there's a right way to say things and a wrong way.

Even when you are in heated discussion with your boss, who is your superior and the person who can potentially make or break your career, take the high road. It's fine to stand your ground to a point, but you need to learn what that point is, and not go beyond it. It is also fine to reiterate the boss's position, and balance his or her perspective in the course of your communication.

Everyone loses their temper now and then. It's inevitable. But take control of the situation and of your emotions. Stop, take a deep breath, and count slowly to five. This simple yet mindful step brings calmness to your mind. In that moment you can remind yourself that "All is well."

Learn to Show Love

We all feel love for someone or something, and love usually occurs many times over during the course of our lifetimes.

Our first love is for our mother and father, the first people we meet and know in this world, the ones who love us back unconditionally, who care for us and raise us into adulthood. As a child, we may not recognize the emotion of love itself, but it is there.

Our next love is for our best friend—our "BFF." Growing up, you are inseparable; you tell each other secrets; you laugh together; you cry together—and even years later, no matter where you are in life, she's still your BFF.

As an adult, you love your partner, your spouse, your better half— the one with whom you share the dreams and hopes of your life, for the rest of your life.

Also as an adult, you find love in the wonder of children, whether they are your own or someone else's. You love their innocence, their curiosity, and their open love back to you.

That's a lifetime of love—the feeling that fills our heart, makes us proud, gives us hope and comfort, makes us smile. I bet that, as you read this, you are thinking of the very people in your own life who are the objects of your love.

Again, we *feel* love for so many others who share our life, but do we *show* love? Do we verbally express love? Love is a beautiful emotion, yet some people are shy or uncomfortable or embarrassed to say the words "I love you." Expressing our love, when we are sincere and when we feel it in our hearts, should be easy. And, when we express our love openly, we give another person an opportunity to do the same. (We empower them.)

Understand, I am not advocating you go around and tell every person you encounter that you love them. No. Those would be empty, meaningless words. Practice this with those you truly love. Reassure them daily—and as often as you feel it—that they are special and they are important to you.

Learn *Not* to Show Anger

Just as we can learn to show love, we can learn *not* to show anger. I recognize opportunities present themselves throughout the day for us to get angry or upset. Someone cuts us off in traffic. The express line at the grocery store is anything but express. Your boss or coworker takes credit for a suggestion you made. Your spouse wasn't able to pick up the kids from daycare.

The first thing to do is mentally remove yourself from the situation and realize you had no way of knowing this issue was going to present itself or that you had any way of preventing it. In other words, the matter is out of your control. What *is* in your control, however, is how you react to the situation. In fact, put the onus on yourself to respond appropriately. When you accept and realize that you are the one in control, you will want to act in such a way that lets you put forth your best, most reasonable, most mature self.

> *For every minute you remain angry, you give up sixty seconds of peace of mind.*
> ~ Ralph Waldo Emerson

Spreading and spewing words of anger and frustration toward others is counterproductive, no matter what the situation. Don't look at the person's bad side. And while you may have just had a glimpse of it, don't focus on it. Quickly think of one—just one—positive quality that person possesses, and focus on that. See how quickly you will have lowered your own blood pressure and defused the situation for yourself.

I learned a valuable lesson from my mother many years ago, and I practice it to this day: If you don't have anything nice to say, don't say anything at all.

It is so much better to exchange words of love than words of anger. Imagine how much less stress and hatred there would be in the world if we all practiced expressing our sincere love more often and more openly.

Learn to Forgive

The act of forgiving is powerful.

Forgiving is important—both for you and for the other person. Learn to forgive others who have done you harm. If you think you cannot forgive someone for their wrong, the situation will eat away at you and cause you unnecessary stress. In fact, only person will lose sleep at night over the situation, and that is you. By focusing only on the negative and not proactively forgiving, an obstacle lies in front of you that negatively affects your ability to manifest what you desire in life.

You don't gain anything by holding a grudge. No matter how right you think you are or how wrong you think the other person is, no matter how difficult, you need to rise above the fray and focus on all the good things in your life. Things will get better.

> *The weak can never forgive. Forgiveness is the attribute of the strong.*
> *~ Mahatma Gandhi*

When you forgive, a weight lifts from your heart and your shoulders. You then become able to move on and focus on more important things. Focus on the here and now, and think about what you can do today to make a better tomorrow for yourself.

Sometimes, the one person who needs forgiving the most is you. I learned this lesson the hard way just three years ago. We had accumulated debt in the six figures. I was very down, very negative at the time. I blamed myself for our situation. Then I did something simple: I forgave myself for my actions that resulted in my family's financial hardship.

Yes, I found the strength to forgive myself, recognizing that what had happened was in the past and that I was unable to go back and start all over again. I realized I needed to stop blaming myself, and to look forward and move forward. I looked for the path that allowed me to make my wrongs right.

So, when you are distraught and wracked with guilt over some situation you may have caused or made worse, don't waste another minute on those emotions. Learn to forgive yourself for whatever it is and move on. When you do that, you will have taken an important step on the road to success and on enjoying future successes in your life.

L is for *Learn*. When people witness or experience something fresh and original, they sometimes say, "You learn something new every day." That's good. But from my perspective, I can only wish for your own betterment—and your ability to teach and attract others—that you learn more than just one new thing each day. Never stop learning. Knowledge and positive emotions are facilitators on your way to attracting wealth.

A
Attract

The eighth and final letter in the word *umbrella* is the letter *A*. In our figurative umbrella of positivity and wisdom, A stands for *Attract*.

Attract: to cause to approach or adhere; to pull or draw to oneself.

Magnets attract. People are attracted to other people. Some attractions are natural, which means they just happen. Others require focus, attention and discipline to work to the degree you want.

Here I discuss what you can do to attract wealth, success, and all that you want in life. I base my suggestions on information I gleaned from Dan Kennedy's *No B.S. Guide to Wealth Attraction for Entrepreneurs*.

Attract Wealth

I think it's a fair statement to say we all want to attract wealth. Well, if you ask for wealth, you will get it. Place your order now for wealth, and you will receive it. You have the power to act in a way that builds and attracts wealth. You have complete control over your finances, so make them work for you. My advice? If you want to attract wealth, act wealthy.

> *Believe you can and you're halfway there.*
> *~ Theodore Roosevelt*

I say this somewhat tongue in cheek. Maybe you've attended a webinar or seminar, or heard speakers who recommend that you buy a new car and new clothes, and start living the life of the rich and famous. Their theory is that, if you pretend you are rich, money will follow. If you live as though you are rich, riches and money and a wealthy lifestyle will follow.

I am here to tell you that pretending you are rich does not make you rich. Riches and wealth do not happen just because you wear designer clothes and drive an expensive car. The only thing that happens is that you bankrupt yourself. And when that happens, the lawyers are the only ones who make any money.

What do I mean when I say that to attract wealth you need to act wealthy? Let's start with the logical step, which takes 90 days to complete. I can tell you it works. This step requires you to open a new bank account. Call it your wealth bank account. Every time you make some money or collect a paycheck, the requirement is that you pay yourself first. Deposit 10% of what you earn into that account. Regardless of your financial status, deposit 10% of your pay, even if it's only fifty cents.

When you put money into a wealth account, it changes you. The act of making that deposit, of paying yourself, makes its way into your subconscious mind and helps you feel better and more positive. Again, save 10% off the top of your earnings for a 90-day period and you will see results. Don't give up on it. In fact, deposit as often as you can.

The apparently illogical step involves opening a second bank account at the same time you open your wealth account. Call this second account your giving account. The deposits you make into this account will be whatever percentage of your wealth account deposits that works for you. Even if your deposit into the giving account is just a few cents, do it. When you do, you will see how your soul, your spirit and mind, are affected in a positive way. You will instantaneously feel better about yourself.

And, as you make deposits in your wealth account, make just as many in your giving account. Over time, your giving value will increase, and eventually enable you to write a check to your favorite charity or church. Or you might give a generous tip to a server or other hard-

Attract

working person. The lesson to be learned here is to always be giving with your money.

Initially, this didn't make sense to me. I soon learned that when you give, you get back what you give four times. Consider my story as an example. In 2012, I formed a group. The group had no specific name or direction, other than the fact that I wanted to help women. I wanted to empower them, the help them succeed and to get somewhere in life.

Helping women is my passion, and I would not charge any woman a dime to be part of this group. I simply wanted to live my passion, to give and share my knowledge and my tools. I had no funds to keep my group going, as I was struggling in my online perfume business and had just recently gotten out of some of our debt. All I knew was that I wanted to do something—anything—to help other women.

My husband supported me, even though our financial situation was not good. He never said no. We brainstormed all sorts of ideas and means to obtain the financial resources I needed to keep my women's group afloat. And we did it. We managed to find money to support my women's empowerment group, in spite of the fact we were barely supporting ourselves and our children. The idea we came up with was to use some of the money from our online perfume sales business, Grand Perfumes. We decided to use the money made from online perfume sales in Wisconsin, which is where we were living at the time. Understand, the majority of our sales were coming from out of state and overseas, as we no longer had a brick-and-mortar store. But, we made the decision that, going forward, a percentage of our online sales in Wisconsin would go toward my group, A Woman's Journey. And so, my own giving program commenced.

At first, my women's group was small—just four members—and a bit depressing. I was happy to get smiles back from women in return for my efforts to launch larger group gatherings and meetings. In time, however, the group grew to 20, then to 200, then 500, and today, there are nearly 900 women in the group—all like-minded women who make things happen.

These women, the dedicated members of A Woman's Journey, all want to be successful. They attend the group's networking sessions regularly and, in fact, would not miss them. They all act in such a way as to attract wealth. What thrills me the most and makes me the proudest is that the members of my group all believe in and adhere to the *UMBRELLA* program. Because of this, I have received a valuable return on my initial investment in this group.

I have been acting in a way so as to attract wealth. I am doing what I love. I am passionate about my work, and it shows. My success is apparent, as is my happiness in what I do. How can I not share my own fortune with others?

Attract Abundance

Once you are on your way to attracting wealth, think about attracting abundance. You may be asking: An abundance of what? *Abundance* and *plenty* mean different things to different people. Think about what you need to be successful and to have a fulfilled life. Choose your own definition of abundance without relying on anyone else's.

Abundance can refer to wealth, as discussed in the previous section. Abundance can mean having a happy family all the time. Abundance can be making health your priority and maintaining good health at all times.

I recognize that my life is overflowing with an abundance of what I need to be successful and filled with joy. I have the most amazing husband in the world; I have the best children a parent could ask for; I have two very successful businesses; I have a successful women's group that I built myself and that puts lots of smiles on people's faces. And I am abundantly happy in that I love what I am privileged to be able to do every day.

A is for *Attract*. When you know exactly what you want, you can give it the right kind of attention. And with proper attention, you will *achieve* results. You will *attract* the results you want. You must, of

Attract

course, be open to receiving these results, and prepared to receive them.

As successes and results come in, celebrate them and keep the positive flow and momentum moving in your direction.

> *Health is the greatest gift, contentment the greatest wealth, faithfulness the best relationship.*
> *~ Buddha*

The Big Picture

An umbrella protects us and shields us from harmful or dangerous elements. Under our literal umbrella we remain dry and sheltered. Under our figurative umbrella, we are protected from negativity, pessimism, and hurtful words and actions. Our umbrella encourages us to shine and motivates us to succeed. Imagine your own umbrella in any color you like, or maybe even a multitude of colors, all reflective of the beauty and uniqueness that is you.

U - Understand

M - Manage

B - Build

R - Remove

E - Empower

L - Listen

L - Learn

A - Attract

About Ami Ahuja

Ami was born and raised in India. Inspired by Mother Teresa and by seeing the hardships women face, she has always wanted to help other women improve their lives. At the age of 20, she moved to the United States and worked three jobs simultaneously to support her parents and siblings.

She met and married Sonny, and joined him in his perfume business, which they grew from two to five physical locations and a distribution center. In addition to doing multiple trade shows every year, they went international with the launch of their website www.GrandPerfumes.com.

Ami is truly passionate about helping women succeed and have a better life. In 2011, she started A Woman's Journey, a women's group where members learn from each other and experts share their knowledge. Learn more at: www.TheBeautifulWomen.org. Ami is also a board-certified Law of Attraction Advanced Practitioner. Today she has thousands of followers on Twitter and Facebook.

Of note, Ami became the first Indian American in history to compete in the Mrs. Wisconsin USA contest, and by winning runner-up, Best Photogenic People's Choice, and Best Photogenic Judges' Choice.

Ami has been featured in national publications such as: *All You, She Magazine, Desi Talk, Indian reporter, Friday Girl TV*.

Ami not only talks the talk but walks the walk with her persuasion in helping others. She goes beyond the call to devote her time, energy, money and resources in support of her community. In her own words, Ami says, "Life is tough, but we can make it better for each other."

Have you visited www.AmiAhuja.com yet to download your free copy of "7 Ways to Remove Negativity"?

www.ingramcontent.com/pod-product-compliance
Lightning Source LLC
Chambersburg PA
CBHW060721030426
42337CB00017B/2960